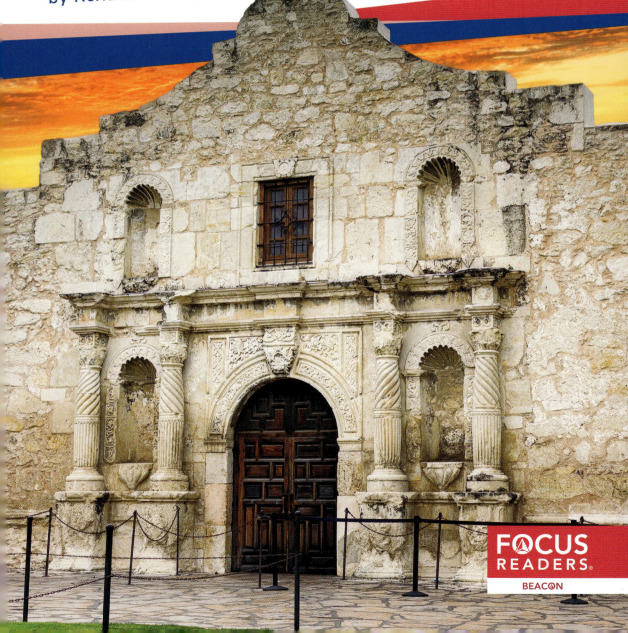

Visit and Learn
The Alamo

by Roxanne Troup

www.focusreaders.com

Copyright © 2024 by Focus Readers®, Lake Elmo, MN 55042. All rights reserved. No part of this book may be reproduced or utilized in any form or by any means without written permission from the publisher.

Focus Readers is distributed by North Star Editions:
sales@northstareditions.com | 888-417-0195

Produced for Focus Readers by Red Line Editorial.

Photographs ©: Shutterstock Images, cover, 1, 4, 7, 11, 16, 19, 21, 22, 25, 27, 29; Austin's Colony, Settlement of/Accession ID: CHA 1989.064/Courtesy State Preservation Board, Austin, TX/Original Artist: McArdle, Henry A./1836-1908/Photographer: Perry Huston, 1/5/95 Post Conservation, 8; North Wind Picture Archives/Alamy, 12; Seguín, Juan Nepomuceno/Accession ID: CHA 1989.096/Courtesy State Preservation Board/Original Artist: Wright, Thomas Jefferson/1798-1846/Photographer: Perry Huston, 7/28/95 post conservation, 14–15

Library of Congress Cataloging-in-Publication Data
Names: Troup, Roxanne, author.
Title: The Alamo / by Roxanne Troup.
Description: Lake Elmo, MN: Focus Readers, [2024] | Series: Visit and
   learn | Includes bibliographical references and index. | Audience:
   Grades 2-3
Identifiers: LCCN 2022062087 (print) | LCCN 2022062088 (ebook) | ISBN
   9781637396131 (hardcover) | ISBN 9781637396704 (paperback) | ISBN
   9781637397800 (ebook pdf) | ISBN 9781637397275 (ebook other)
Subjects: LCSH: Alamo (San Antonio, Tex.)--Juvenile literature. | Alamo
   (San Antonio, Tex.)--Siege, 1836--Juvenile literature. |
   Texas--History--To 1846--Juvenile literature. | San Antonio
   (Tex.)--Buildings, structures, etc.--Juvenile literature.
Classification: LCC F390.T76 2024 (print) | LCC F390 (ebook) | DDC
   976.4/03--dc23/eng/20221230
LC record available at https://lccn.loc.gov/2022062087
LC ebook record available at https://lccn.loc.gov/2022062088

Printed in the United States of America
Mankato, MN
082023

About the Author

Author of more than a dozen books for kids, Roxanne Troup writes engaging nonfiction for all ages. She lives in the mountains of Colorado and loves visiting state and national parks to hike with her family. She also enjoys visiting schools to promote literacy and teach about writing.

Table of Contents

CHAPTER 1
A Long History 5

CHAPTER 2
A Battle for Texas 9

THAT'S AMAZING!
Juan Seguín 14

CHAPTER 3
Remembering the Alamo 17

CHAPTER 4
Visiting the Alamo 23

Focus on the Alamo • 28
Glossary • 30
To Learn More • 31
Index • 32

Chapter 1

A Long History

An old building stands in downtown San Antonio, Texas. Its walls are made of pale stone. They block the hot sun. People crowd the area. They learn about the building's past.

The Alamo's walls are limestone.

The Alamo started out as a Spanish **mission**. It was founded in 1718. Missionaries lived inside the Alamo's walls. They wanted to convert **Indigenous** peoples to Christianity. They also taught Spanish to Indigenous

Many people think the Alamo is only one building. However, the original mission included living areas. It also had storage rooms.

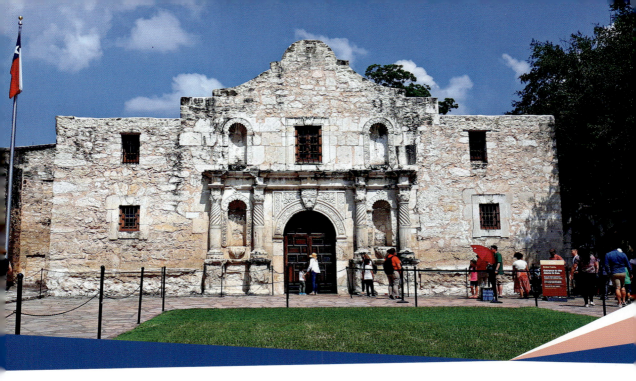

 The Alamo was first known as the Mission San Antonio de Valero.

peoples. They taught farming and weaving, too.

The mission closed in 1793. The building stayed empty for several years. But in the early 1800s, it became a Spanish fort.

Chapter 2

A Battle for Texas

In the 1820s, Texas was part of Mexico. During this time, many settlers moved to Texas. Very few of them were Mexican. Most were from the United States. These settlers were known as Texians.

 Many Texians used violence to take over the lands of Indigenous peoples.

Antonio López de Santa Anna became Mexico's president in 1833. Santa Anna did not trust the Texians. He feared they would make Texas part of the United States.

Santa Anna changed Mexico's laws. He gave more power to the national government. As a result, Texas had less power. Texians hated this change. They started to **rebel**. The Texas Revolution had begun.

Santa Anna sent soldiers to Texas. The Texians won a few small

 Santa Anna served as Mexico's president several times during his long career.

battles. However, Santa Anna kept going toward San Antonio. Most Texian soldiers left the city. But a small group moved into the Alamo. They prepared to fight.

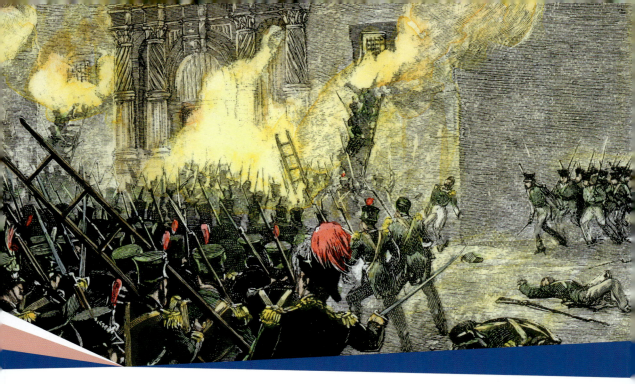

 An old drawing shows Santa Anna's soldiers attacking the Alamo.

Santa Anna attacked the Alamo in March 1836. He had more than 2,000 soldiers. The Texians had fewer than 200. Santa Anna took no prisoners. His soldiers killed all the Texian fighters inside.

In April, the two armies met again. This time, they were in southeast Texas. The Texians remembered Santa Anna's cruelty at the Alamo. The Texians won the battle. Texas was now free of Mexican control. It became an **independent** country.

Texas remained independent for nearly 10 years. Then, in 1845, it joined the United States.

THAT'S AMAZING!

Juan Seguín

Juan Seguín was a Tejano. That is the name for Mexican settlers in Texas. Like many people in Texas, he did not trust Santa Anna. Seguín thought Texas should be independent. So, in 1835, he joined the Texian army.

Seguín was at the Alamo when Santa Anna arrived. But he left town to deliver a message. He told Texian leaders to send more soldiers. While Seguín was away, the Alamo fell to Santa Anna.

Seguín kept fighting for Texas. He took part in the battle that defeated Santa Anna. Seguín helped Texas win its independence.

Juan Seguín became mayor of San Antonio in 1833.

Chapter 3

Remembering the Alamo

The Alamo means different things to different people. For some, it is a symbol of **patriotism**. The soldiers who defended the Alamo loved their country. They were also trying to protect their home.

 A painting from the early 1900s shows Texians fighting bravely.

The Texian soldiers knew they could not win the battle. But they fought anyway.

Others see the Alamo as a symbol of slavery. Many Texians brought enslaved people into Texas. At first, Mexico let them. But later, the law changed. Slavery was no longer allowed in Mexico. This change made many Texians angry. They wanted to keep slavery legal. Slavery was one of the causes of the Texas Revolution.

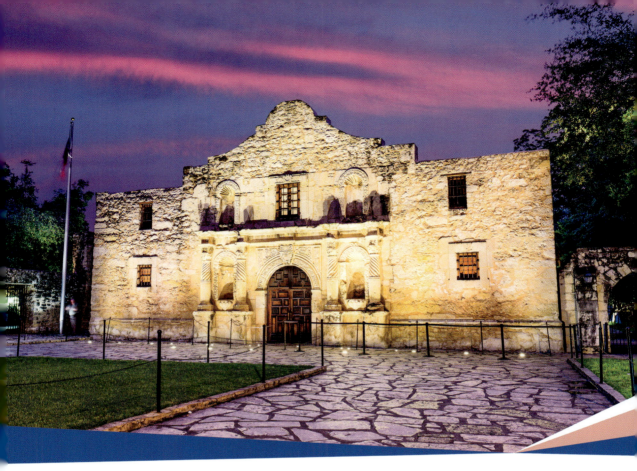

 Today, people continue to debate whether the Alamo site should mention slavery.

People also see the Alamo as part of imperialism. Imperialism is a way of spreading a country's power. It often involves violence.

It also involves taking over land. For instance, many European countries expanded by creating **colonies**. Later, the United States expanded by moving into the West. Settlers in Texas were part of this process. They hoped to spread US **influence**.

Texas soldiers fought in the Mexican-American War (1846–1848). They used the battle cry "Remember the Alamo!"

 Some actors at the Alamo dress as Mexican soldiers.

Today, the Alamo reminds visitors about all these ideas. It honors people of many backgrounds who lived, worked, and died there. The Alamo shows visitors that history can be complicated. Even so, history needs to be remembered.

Chapter 4

Visiting the Alamo

Millions of people visit the Alamo every year. Many visitors are surprised at its size. The Alamo is small. Much of its original structure is gone. Only the chapel and part of the living area remain.

 The living area is known as the Long Barrack. It is the oldest part of the Alamo.

The city of San Antonio has been built up around it.

Most visitors take tours. Guides walk people through the area. They share the Alamo's history. They tell battle stories. Some of these stories cannot be proven. They might be **myths**. Some visitors take audio tours. They listen to the Alamo story while music and battle sounds play.

The Alamo has several outdoor exhibits, too. Visitors can see a

 San Antonio is working to restore the Alamo's grounds. The city wants visitors to see how the area looked in the 1800s.

cannon. They can see a defensive wall made of logs. They can watch living history **demonstrations**. Actors wear clothes from the 1830s. They show visitors how people lived back then.

On weekends, actors shoot old rifles in the street. But they do not use real bullets. Visitors get to see, hear, and smell what the Battle of the Alamo was like.

After the tour, visitors walk through the Alamo's museum. It shows many objects and

Did You Know?

The Alamo also offers virtual tours. That way, people who can't visit in person can still experience it.

 Actors show visitors what the battle may have looked like.

documents. For instance, soldiers' uniforms are on display. Visitors can also see guns and cannonballs. The museum helps people learn the history of the Alamo.

FOCUS ON
The Alamo

Write your answers on a separate piece of paper.

1. Write a paragraph explaining the main ideas of Chapter 3.

2. What does the Alamo mean to you? Why?

3. What type of place was the Alamo when it was first built?
   - **A.** a mission
   - **B.** a fort
   - **C.** a museum

4. Why did Santa Anna attack the Alamo?
   - **A.** He thought the Texian soldiers would give up.
   - **B.** He wanted to help the Texians form a new country.
   - **C.** He didn't want Texians to break away from Mexico.

5. What does **founded** mean in this book?

*The Alamo started out as a Spanish mission. It was **founded** in 1718.*

   A. discovered something new
   B. officially started
   C. learned about religion

6. What does **exhibits** mean in this book?

*The Alamo has several outdoor **exhibits**, too. Visitors can see a cannon.*

   A. places that are easy to get to
   B. displays that people can look at
   C. weapons that people can fight with

Answer key on page 32.

Glossary

colonies
Areas controlled by a country that is far away.

demonstrations
Events that teach people how something works or how something was done in the past.

independent
Able to make decisions without being controlled by another government.

Indigenous
Native to a region, or belonging to ancestors who lived in a region before colonists arrived.

influence
The power to affect what other people do or think.

mission
A settlement set up by a church to expand its religion.

myths
Well-known stories that may not be completely true.

patriotism
A strong love for one's country.

rebel
To fight against the people who are in charge.

To Learn More

BOOKS

Huddleston, Emma. *Exploring the San Antonio River Walk*. Lake Elmo, MN: Focus Readers, 2020.

Otfinoski, Steven. *The Battle of the Alamo: Texans Under Siege*. North Mankato, MN: Capstone Press, 2019.

Rea, Amy C. *The Battle of the Alamo Ignites Independence*. Mankato, MN: The Child's World, 2019.

NOTE TO EDUCATORS

Visit **www.focusreaders.com** to find lesson plans, activities, links, and other resources related to this title.

Index

A
actors, 25–26

C
chapel, 23
colonies, 20

E
exhibits, 24–25

I
imperialism, 19–20
Indigenous peoples, 6–7

M
Mexican-American War, 20
mission, 6–7
museum, 26–27

P
patriotism, 17

S
San Antonio, 5, 11, 14, 24
Santa Anna, Antonio López de, 10–13, 14
Seguín, Juan, 14
slavery, 18

T
Texas Revolution, 10, 18
Texians, 9–13, 14, 18
tours, 24, 26

V
visitors, 21, 23–27

Answer Key: 1. Answers will vary; **2.** Answers will vary; **3.** A; **4.** C; **5.** B; **6.** B